POLICE TECHNOLOGIES

FOR PLACE-BASED

CRIME PREVENTION

::

INTEGRATING

RISK TERRAIN MODELING

FOR ACTIONABLE INTEL

By

Eric L. Piza

I0415276

On Behalf Of

The Rutgers Center on Public Security

in partial fulfillment of NIJ Grant 2016-IJ-CX-K001

(Co-Principal Investigators Leslie W. Kennedy and Joel M. Caplan)

RUTGERS
Center on Public Security

Issues in Spatial Analysis Series, Vol. 1

Edited by J. M. Caplan and L. W. Kennedy

2019

Newark, New Jersey

USA

Suggested Citation

Piza, E. L. (2019). *Issues in Spatial Analysis Series: Vol. 1. Police Technologies for Place-Based Crime Prevention: Integrating Risk Terrain Modeling for Actionable Intel*. Newark, NJ: Rutgers Center on Public Security.

Produced by the Rutgers Center on Public Security

Based at Rutgers University's School of Criminal Justice, the Rutgers Center on Public Security (RCPS) offers a multidisciplinary approach to the academic study and practical application of ways in which democratic societies can effectively address crime, terrorism and other threats to public security. This involves the prevention of, protection from and response to natural or man-made events that could endanger the safety or security of people or property in a given area. RCPS engages in innovative data analysis and information dissemination, including the use of GIS, for strategic decision-making and tactical action.

Visit www.rutgerscps.org

CONTENTS

PREFACE

Risk-Terrain Modeling (RTM) is a place-based crime forecasting technique that diagnoses spatial risk factors of criminal behavior. It emphasizes micro places where multiple significant risk factors co-locate (Caplan, Kennedy, & Miller, 2011). Findings of RTM analyses allow researchers to make accurate predictions about the micro-places where crime is likely to occur in the future while also providing important context regarding the environmental backcloth (Brantingham & Brantingham, 1993) of high-crime places.

RTM has been used in the development of Risk-Based Policing, which emphasizes designing and implementing police interventions that directly target spatial risk factors that contribute to the emergence and persistence of crime hot spots. Risk-based policing helps build upon traditional place-based approaches to crime by not only identifying micro-places most likely to experience crime, but helping police stay constantly attuned to the dynamic patterns and attractors of crime (Kennedy, Caplan, & Piza, 2018: 35).

In observing the benefits RTM has provided to spatial analysis and place-based policing, this report considers the potential benefits RTM can provide to common crime control technologies: CCTV video surveillance cameras, police body-worn cameras, and gunshot detection systems. Research has highlighted pertinent issues inherent in each of these technologies. The report explores the ways that RTM may help improve upon the efficiency and effectiveness of each technology. Additionally, in recognition of the rich data that police technologies generate on a continuous basis, the report explores how integration of RTM with police technologies may help in the further development of RTM and Risk-Based Policing.

This report points to a number of key takeaways, including:

- Contemporary police technologies are predominately deployed in a "black box" manner with little known about the processes and mechanisms necessary to achieved the desired effect. RTM stands out in contrast to other technologies.

- RTM may help to provide the type of "bright data" necessary to maximize the effect of police technologies.

- RTM can be used for closed-circuit television (CCTV) camera site suitability assessments and optimal installation locations.
- RTM can be used to prioritize police body-worn camera (BWC) deployments to maximize the immediate impact.
- Video footage generated by CCTV and BWCs can help to identify pertinent spatial risk factors for RTM, and to better understand causal mechanisms and crime risk narratives for effective risk-based policing activities.
- CCTV and BWCs can be used to identify police officer actions that effectively mitigate risky places and situations.
- RTM can be used to maximize effects of gunshot detection systems (GDS) by identifying the micro-places most at-risk of future shooting events as optimal target areas.
- RTM can be used to identify areas where installation of acoustic sensors for GDS should be avoided to minimize the potential for false positive gunfire events detected.
- RTM allows for less expensive deployments of GDS while still achieving optimal impact.

- The research literature provides evidence-based insight into the types of methodologies needed to support the various RTM-technology integrations discussed in this report.

CHAPTER 1
THE INFLUENCE OF TECHNOLOGY IN POLICING

Throughout history, the introduction of technology has directly driven the evolution of policing. The early 1900's, which police historians consider the start of American policing's professional era (Miller, 1977), saw a great deal of technological innovation, such as the mass production of automobiles and household telephones, that transformed society. Similar to the general citizenry, police began to make use of these new technologies in their day-to-day functions. However, it would be wrong to consider these technologies simply as tools that police incorporate in their mission. Rather, these technologies, in many ways, directly influenced the operational priorities of policing (Kennedy, Caplan, & Piza, 2018: 14-15). Automobile patrol replaced foot patrol as the main operational strategy of police. At the same time, the advent of the 9-1-1 emergency line and two-way radios made the rapid response to citizen calls for service a top priority of American policing. The benefits provided by these technologies, specifically the "omnipresence" offered by widespread motor vehicle patrol and perceived instantaneous closures of crime offered by rapid response (Wilson, 1963), shaped policing throughout the 1990s and, arguably, remain the cornerstones of most police agencies in present day (Mastrofski & Willis, 2011).

Over time, the benefits of the professional era's primary strategies of omnipresence and rapid response would be rebuked. Declining public confidence in the police, combined with an influx of research finding little effect of these strategies, led to a re-consideration of the police mission (Weisburd and Braga, 2006). By the turn of the 20th century, the standard model would be de-emphasized by contemporary police scholars and innovative police managers in favor of strategies collectively known as the "focused" (Skogan and Frydl, 2004) or "customized" (Sherman, 2011) model of policing. Whereas the standard model relied on reactive responses to committed crime, this new police paradigm emphasizes proactive police activities and a diversity of approaches for the purpose of preventing crime (Lum, Koper, & Telep, 2011; Weisburd & Eck, 2004).

The range of policing strategies falling within the focused/customized framework requires a degree of analytical precision for police agencies. Such analysis involves quantitative predictions of where and when crime is most likely to occur (Sherman, 2011) as well as theoretical understanding of the causal mechanisms underlying crime patterns (Eck, 2006; Sampson, Winship, & Knight, 2013) for the purpose of customizing strategies to fit the local context. Such practices have been facilitated by the increased availability of analytical software such as geographic information systems and quantitative analysis products. In this manner, crime analysis is a staple of modern policing.

Certain strategies, such as hot spots policing or problem-oriented policing, simply cannot occur without some level of crime analysis. Crime analysis is also essential for other policing strategies, such as problem-oriented policing, focused deterrence, and CompStat (Santos, 2014). In recognizing the importance of crime analysis in contemporary policing, scholars have argued that policing would benefit from an expanded role of crime analysts to include functions such as program evaluation (Piza & Feng, 2017) and translation of research into practice for police managers (Lum & Koper, 2017). In sum, it is clear that crime analysts are key contributors to evidence-based policing.

The continued development of technology has contributed to the further evolution of the police mission. The integration of disparate technologies and associated data systems has pushed policing into a new era, where "big data" is central to the day-to-day functions of policing (Ferguson, 2017; Kennedy et al., 2018). Data are made "big" due to the expanding police apparatus that includes many more sources of information than before. While crime analysis has traditionally included information on crime incidents and officer actions (e.g. arrests, stops, and citations), data from police technologies such as video surveillance cameras, gunshot detection systems, body-worn cameras, and scanners greatly increase the amount of information at the disposal of the police.

The shift towards this style of policing warrants discussion, particularly in terms of the societal consequences of policing based on "big data." Appropriately, a large proportion of such discussion relates to privacy and civil liberty concerns, which has been covered in-depth elsewhere (e.g. Ferguson, 2017). However, also important is the notion of whether the manner by which big data and the associated technologies actually generate the anticipated public safety benefits. The adoption of technology in policing has arguably created what Norris & Armstrong (1999: 9) refer to as "technological determinism" which they define as "an unquestioning belief in the power of technology." While Norris & Armstrong (1999) made this observation in regards to CCTV surveillance cameras, such technological determinism can negatively affect the deployment of any police technology. Despite representing "innovation" within policing, many technologies have primarily been deployed in a manner that supports traditional and reactive police strategies (Lum, Koper, & Willis, 2017). Given the large body of research showing that reactive strategies have little crime control benefit, the adoption of technology can have the unintended consequence of undermining an agency's objectives for adopting a given technology (Lum et al., 2017).

Ferguson's (2017) critique of "big data" policing helps to shed some light on the paradoxical situation of technology adoptions which are meant to improve police operations yielding the opposite, deleterious, effects. Ferguson (2017: p. 3) argued that big data policing largely revolves around what he refers to as "black data," meaning the data is opaque, largely hidden within complex algorithms and societal tendencies to view anything described as "data-driven" as legitimate, even in the absence of observable outcomes in support of this assertion. Extending Ferguson's argument of "black data" to the technologies that produce such information helps to explain how technology can too often fall short (or even sabotage) its intended objectives.

CHAPTER 2
MAXIMIZING TECHNOLOGY IN POLICING: HOW TO MOVE FORWARD

While highlighting the significant threats posed by "black data", Ferguson (2017) does not dismiss big data in policing outright. Rather, he highlights the promise of what he refers to as "bright data," which uses information gained from the police's technological architecture to address environmental and social risks. Ferguson (2017: 167) argued data can be "bright" in the sense they are smart (precise and focused) and illuminating (revealing hidden problems and patterns).

In illustrating the potential benefits of bright data, Ferguson (2017) discussed the risk-based policing intervention conducted in Colorado Springs, CO (Kennedy, Caplan, & Piza, 2018). The Colorado Springs Police Department (CSPD) partnered with Kennedy and colleagues to conduct an RTM analysis to (1) identify spatial risk factors for motor vehicle theft and (2) design a risk-based policing intervention that directly addressed the spatial influence of the targeted risk factors. The spatial risk factors helped shed light on not only the motor vehicle theft hot spots in the city, but *why* these places were high-crime. For example, apartment complexes with large parking lots provided a rich number of targets (i.e. cars) not visible from the apartments while cars nearby restaurants are similarly out of the view of owners for considerable periods of time. Furthermore, the presence of crime attractors such as convenience stores and gas stations can provide motivated offenders a level of "deniability" that allows them to blend-in at particular areas for extended periods of time (Piza, Feng, Kennedy, & Caplan, 2017). Ferguson (2017) noted that the "bright data" offering such insights into the environmental features giving rise to motor vehicle theft hot spots allows for targeted interventions to include a range of preventative activities that move beyond traditional law enforcement activities. Indeed, CSPD's risk-based policing intervention included a range of activities outside of law enforcement, including neighborhood blight cleanups and community meetings.

Ferguson's (2017) concept can be expanded to the use of technology in policing generally. When looking at the typical manner by which research and evaluation of criminal justice technology is conducted, and the data generated by such efforts, the field seems to be operating somewhat in the "black." The emergence of the evidence-based policing movement has increased calls for the use of scientific evidence in the development of crime control practices. Scholars have argued that evidence-based policing parallels evidence-based medicine, given the emphasis on employing rigorous research findings in policy decisions (Sherman, 1998). However, others have argued that such a description of medical research is narrow given the full range of considerations involved in medical treatment (Greene, 2014; Sparrow, 2011). In addition to desired outcomes (i.e., whether a given treatment effectively cured the health ailment) medical research uses multiple methodological and interpretive approaches to explain procedural aspects of treatment such as physician-client interaction, unintended side effects, and the practice of treatment delivery (Greene, 2014).

When considering medical research through this lens, evidence-based policing somewhat pales in comparison. Evidence-based crime prevention primarily concerns itself with the methodological strength of research evaluations, with stronger designs helping to ensure the level of internal validity needed to determine that the observed treatment led to changes in crime levels rather than a range of plausible alternate hypotheses (Farrington, Gottfredson, Sherman, and Welsh, 2002). While this is obviously an important consideration, whether a program succeeds in preventing crime is only one of a range of important considerations for crime control policy. In particular, the casual mechanisms of effective policy as well as procedural considerations in successfully implementing said policy are important considerations for practitioners (Salvemini, Piza, Carter, Grommon, & Merritt, 2015; Sampson et al., 2013). Unfortunately, such factors are often not measured in evaluations of crime prevention programs (Eck, 2006).

The issue of exclusively focusing on outcomes to the detriment of procedural and contextual considerations is heightened in the case of criminal justice technology. This is especially the case given that the procedural aspects of technology are highly interrelated, with latter tasks contingent on the successful completion of earlier tasks. Salvemini et al. (2015: 313) illustrated this point through the example of CCTV video surveillance, which requires "(1) installation of cameras which have a continuous connection to electricity and a hardwired or wireless telecommunications network, (2) continuous relay of video footage from the cameras to a central station, (3) retroactive or real-time video footage monitoring by a human operator, (4) detection of criminal infractions contained in the footage by the operator, (5) notification of the police of the criminal infraction, and (6) on-site or post investigation apprehension by the police of the offender (either on scene or at a later date following an investigation) observed committing the criminal infraction (LaVigne, Lowry, Markman, & Dwyer, 2011; Ratcliffe, 2006)." As this example describes, outcomes of crime control technology are largely a part of human and system performance, operational procedures, and policies that direct the technology's usage within a given agency (Salvemini et al., 2015). Unfortunately, for most technologies, research has predominately focused on the outcome effects with important procedural and contextual considerations left unexplored. The end result, seemingly, is police adopting technology while knowing "little about how to use such technologies so that they work best" (Weisburd & Neyroud, 2011: 7).

A review of the typical focus of research on police technology shows how this body of research may disproportionately produce "black data" that does not provide enough insight on how police can optimally leverage said technology. The question, then, is how can technology research and associated data be made "bright?"

As previously discussed, the emergence of new technologies has directly driven the evolution of modern policing. However, when considering the police practices with the most established records of success, the integration of technology alone does not generate positive crime control benefits. Rather, effective strategies are highly focused and commonly incorporate a diversity of tactics (Lum et al., 2011; Weisburd & Eck, 2004). Strong crime analysis capabilities are needed to enable police to achieve the requisite level of focus and to identify the strategies likely to work best in the local context (Clarke & Eck, 2005; Rachel Boba Santos, 2014).

This finding can have important implications for police technology as well. In short, applying crime analysis to understand the causal mechanisms underlying common police technologies and to inform the deployment of technological solutions to crime. Conversely, police technologies may be leveraged in a manner that improves our capacity to conduct rigorous analysis of crime and diagnose casual factors of crime patterns. These ideas are explored further in the next chapter.

CHAPTER 3
CRIME ANALYSIS AND PLACE-BASED POLICING

Crime analysis practices have done much to enhance the effectiveness of modern police practices. A vivid illustration of this can be seen in the example of place-based policing. As recently as the early 1990s, scholars were largely pessimistic about the crime prevention capacity of the police. Bayley (1994: 3) delivered a harshly worded assessment of the research evidence that would become a widely cited rebuke of the police function: "The police do not prevent crime. This is one of the best kept secrets of modern life. Experts know it, the police know it, but the public does not know it. Yet the police pretend that they are society's best defense against crime... This is a myth."

The observations of Bayley (1994), as well as other scholars espousing similar doubts of police effectiveness (Gottfredson & Hirschi, 1990; Klockars, 1983), are based on the inefficiencies of standard law enforcement practices. A vivid illustration of this critique, as well as an example of how crime analysis has helped move the field forward, can be seen in the context of police patrol.

Dating to the beginning of policing's professional era, patrol has been considered "the backbone of policing" with a majority of officers in any given agency assigned to patrol functions on a daily basis (Gaines & Kappeler, 2005: 200). However, while cemented as a main function of police, research has demonstrated little evidence of the benefits of standard police patrol. The limitations of standard patrol, during which police randomly patrolled police beats in an attempt to generate "omnipresence," was demonstrated by the Kansas City Preventive Patrol Experiment (Kelling et al., 1974). Fifteen patrol beats in Kansas City were randomly assigned to receive either increased, decreased, or standard levels of patrol with no significant differences in crime observed across the patrol beats at the conclusion of the experiment. While scholars have noted issues in the design and analysis employed by Kelling et al. (1974) (see, for example, Sherman & Weisburd, 1995), the Kansas City patrol experiment dominated thinking on police patrol in the field, and largely reflects the research evidence showing that the standard model of policing has little effect on crime and disorder (Skogan & Frydl, 2004).

The research evidence on preventative patrol may lead one to the seemingly straightforward conclusions that police patrol does not "work." However, in considering public policy, it is important to not only focus on the pertinent results, but to consider the context and mechanisms that could have influenced the observed outcomes (Sampson, Winship, & Knight, 2013). When analyzed through such a lens, the failure of preventative patrol seems due more to the manner by which the tactic is implemented rather than any inherent limitations in the concept itself (Berman & Fox, 2010). Sherman & Weisburd (1995) argued that police patrol delivered at large geographies such as police beats results in low statistical power and difficulty in measuring precisely how much patrol dosage was delivered to the treated units. Therefore, despite the commonality of police beats as the unit of treatment, patrol delivered at such a level is unlikely to generate any significant crime control benefits (Weisburd, 2008)

As described by Sherman & Weisburd (1995: 629), spreading the allocation of patrol across large geographies results in the dilution of the potential deterrent effect of police presence at the individual places that comprise the police beat. Therefore, they advocated, not for the discontinuance of patrol, but for a change in the unit of analysis selected for treatment. In particular, Sherman & Weisburd (1995) argued that patrol activities should be targeted at the micro-places where crimes cluster (i.e. hot spots) as focusing police presence in these concise areas would likely have a greater deterrent effect than spreading patrol thinly across meso- or macro-level geographies. This argument was scientifically informed, reflecting early research demonstrating that a majority of crime clusters in a relatively small number of micro-places (Sherman, Gartin, & Buerger, 1989), a finding that has been replicated in a large number of research since (Lee, Eck, O, & Martinez, 2017).

Sherman & Weisburd's (1995) randomized experiment of organizing patrol around geographic hot spots in Minneapolis generated significant reductions in crime at treatment units as compared to controls, a finding that has been consistently replicated in place-based policing studies (Braga, Papachristos, & Hureau, 2014). A recent simulation study found that focusing police activities at hot spots can have a strong enough effect to generate city-wide crime reductions (Weisburd, Braga, Groff, &

Wooditch, 2017), providing additional support for place-based policing as a crime control policy. In considering the re-operationalization of place, it is again important to consider the role of technology. Identifying significant crime clusters at the micro-level, such as street segments and intersections, is made possible by the availability of GIS and crime mapping technology. The type of micro-level place-based policing that has emerged in recent decades would not have been possible prior to the wide proliferation of GIS technology. As such, prior focus on large geographies may have been more a result of technological limitations as lack of ingenuity on the part of police leaders.

CHAPTER 4
RISK TERRAIN MODELING, RISK-BASED POLICING, AND CRIME CONTROL TECHNOLOGY

Recent advancements in spatial crime analysis have further added to the development of place-based policing. While research has emphasized the identification of micro-level hot spots, with a range of hot spot identification techniques previously developed (see, for example, Haberman, 2017), recent developments in spatial analysis have allowed researchers to diagnose the environmental factors giving rise to hot spots and forecast the micro-places most at-risk of experiencing crime in the future. Risk Terrain Modeling (RTM) is an example of such a technique that has become largely incorporated in place-based policing efforts by law enforcement agencies around the world (Caplan, Kennedy, & Miller, 2011; Caplan & Kennedy, 2016). RTM is a theoretically grounded approach to spatial crime analysis that identifies specific environmental features that generate crime (Caplan & Kennedy, 2016) as well as the unique spatial influence each individual feature exerts on the environmental backcloth (Caplan, 2011).

In their applied partnership with police agencies across the United States, Kennedy et al. (2018) further developed Risk Terrain Modeling to design police interventions in a manner that directly targets spatial risk factors that contribute to the emergence and persistence of crime hot spots (Kennedy, Caplan, Piza, & Buccine-Schraeder, 2016) rather than simply identifying micro-level places as target areas. These risk-based policing efforts were designed in partnership with police leaders through the implementation of the ACTION agenda. The acronym of ACTION represents the steps of risk-governance necessary to synthesize findings of RTM analyses for the purpose of designing place-based policing interventions (Caplan & Kennedy, 2016: 84; Kennedy et al., 2018: 38).

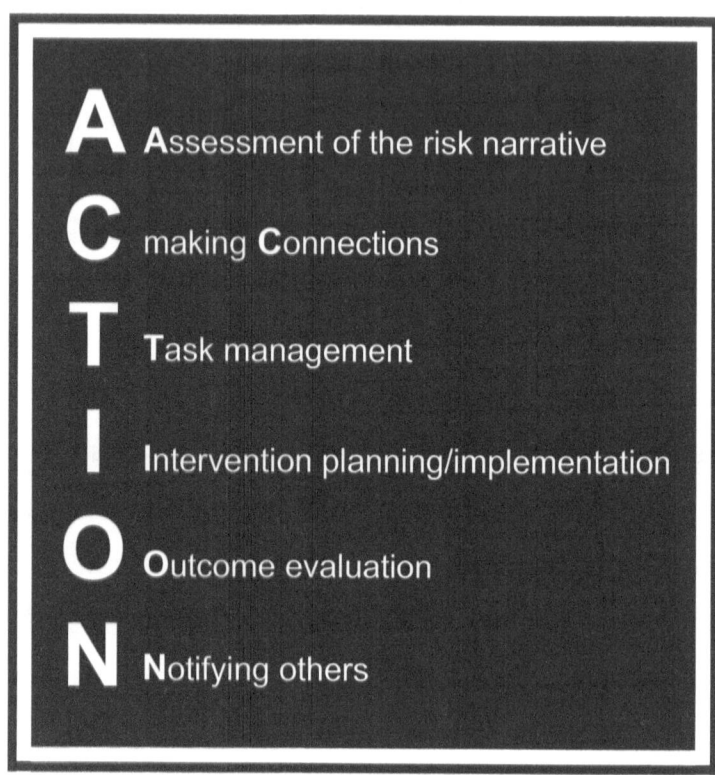

Figure: Overview of ACTION

Figure Source: Caplan, J. M. & Kennedy, L. W. (2016). Risk Terrain Modeling: Crime Prediction and Risk Reduction. Oakland, CA: University of California Press

See also Chapter 4, "Risk-Based Policing and ACTION", in Kennedy, L. W., Caplan, J. M., and Piza, E. L. (2018). Risk-Based Policing: Evidence-Based Crime Prevention with Big Data and Spatial Analytics. Oakland, CA: University of California Press

ACTION meetings enable the police agencies to develop place-based interventions in a manner that directly incorporates spatial risk factors in targeted interventions. For example, in Glendale, AZ, convenience stores were identified as a significant risk factor for robbery. An officer at the ACTION meeting attributed this finding to many convenience stores placing automated cell phone return kiosks in their businesses, where customers could dispose of old cell phones for cash. The officer felt that this provided offenders a way to earn fast cash for cell phones taken during robberies. The crime analysts were able to provide empirical support for this view, with cell phones being taken much more frequently in robberies occurring in close proximity of convenience stores than robberies at other locations in the city (Piza, Kennedy, & Caplan, 2018: 499). This information was used in the design of Glendale PD's risk-based policing intervention, which included directed patrol in areas around convenience stores and officers distributing flyers to pedestrians advising them to take caution when using their personal electronic devices in public.

Similarly, the Newark PD used the findings of their gun violence risk terrain model to design an intervention that generated location checks and manager contacts at three business types: restaurants, food take outs, and gas stations. Each day during the intervention, a task force comprised of three officers under the supervision of a lieutenant visited businesses located within the target area. Upon visiting the business, officers were required to meet with the on-duty manager and have them sign a log sheet to ensure that proper contact was established (Kennedy et al., 2018).

The risk-based policing interventions developed by Kennedy et al. (2018) and their police partners used RTM findings largely to inform the role of personnel in crime prevention efforts: the target areas and intervention activities of patrol and other units of the police agency that should participate in the intervention, for example. However, given the frequency with which police use technology in their crime prevention mission, the possibility exists for insights gleaned from RTM and Risk-based policing to improve upon common deployments of crime control technology. As previously discussed, RTM provided important insights for police to consider during place-based crime control interventions. Given these observations, it is worth considering whether RTM could provide similar insights for the role of technology in crime control. This is particularly the case in light of the fact that, frankly speaking, police use of technology commonly leaves much to be desired.

Through a mixed-method multi-agency study, Lum et al. (2017) found that police view technology through technological and organizational frames defined by traditional and reactive policing approaches. In particular, police officers largely reported that they used technology most often when conducting reactive, standard modes of policing (e.g. during responses to calls for service, while conducting field interviews of suspects, etc.) with proactive, preventative, and community-oriented uses of technology observed rarely. Such use of technology, influenced by the officer's interpretive "frames," can severely hinder the effect of technology as well as their potential for generating true reform. This follows the general research on technology adoption in policing, which suggests new technologies are rarely used to call existing strategies into question, but are rather adapted to support current practices (Manning, 2008).

Given the observations gleaned from risk-based policing efforts (Kennedy et al., 2018; Piza et al., 2018), incorporating RTM in technology-driven police interventions may help to expand the scope (and effectiveness) of contemporary crime control technology. However, in discussing the potential benefits RTM can provide police technology, it is important to note that more creatively leveraging technology may also contribute to the further evolution of RTM.

Despite being developed fairly recently, RTM has been consistently expanded and improved on by its architects. The inaugural RTM analysis conducted by Caplan et al. (2011) operationalized a multi-step process for creating density maps of individual risk factors, summing these disparate density files into a composite risk map assigning a risk value at all micro-places within a study area, and using said risk values to forecast the location of future crime events. Kennedy, Caplan, & Piza (2011) built upon the approach of Caplan et al. (2011) by developing a method of selecting specific risk factors for inclusion in an RTM model and validating a "best model" that most accurately forecasts crime events. The notion of risk factor section and the identification of a best model is helpful for agencies with large amounts of GIS data at their disposal. Caplan & Kennedy (2013) developed the Risk

Terrain Modeling Diagnostics (RTMDx) software to automate the RTM process, including testing the spatial influence of each risk factor at various distances (e.g. up to 4 blocks, in ½ block increments) and selecting the optimal operationalization (i.e. density of features or proximity to features) for inclusion in the best model. More recently, research has improved upon the predictive accuracy of RTM by combing the approach with other spatial analysis methods, such as kernel density estimation (Caplan, Kennedy, Piza, & Barnum, 2019) and near-repeat analysis (Garnier, Caplan, & Kennedy, 2018).

Subsequent evolutions of RTM should likely revolve around shedding light on the context by which risk factors influence the environment. As articulated by Perry, McInnes, Price, Smith, & Hollywood (2013: 55) a primary challenge in place-based crime forecasting is distinguishing spatial risk factors that are truly criminogenic from those that are merely correlated with highly populated areas (meaning there is simply a larger pool of potential targets). Gerell (2018) recently illustrated this challenge in his analysis of spatial risk factors and violence in Malmö, Sweden. Gerell (2018) found that, in a baseline model, restaurants, bars, ATMs, schools, and bus shelters were each positively related to violence crime counts. However, when the count of bus passengers (i.e. the number of targets in an area) was added as an exposure variable, only restaurants retained statistical significance in the full model (see Table 3 in Gerrell, 2018). As noted by Gerrell (2018: 362), this analysis suggests "that some of the risk factors commonly spatially associated with crime largely function through drawing more people to a location" rather than any criminogenic effects they impart on the surrounding area.

As will be discussed in the subsequent chapter, mining the outputs of many common police technologies can provide the type of data necessary to shed light on the causal mechanisms by which spatial risk factors increase the likelihood of crime. In this sense, the "bright" data (Ferguson, 2017) that RTM can offer police technology may flow in the opposite direction as well; data generated by contemporary police technology can help inform the further development of RTM.

It is with these issues in mind that the remainder of the report is focused. The subsequent chapters focus on 3 technologies prominent in contemporary policing: CCTV surveillance cameras, police body-worn cameras, and gunshot detection systems. Each chapter provides an overview of the technology, including pertinent limitations identified in the literature. The discussion then proceeds to how RTM may be able to improve upon the efficiency and effectiveness of the technology. Each chapter concludes with a discussion of how information generated by the technology may help isolate the causal mechanisms underlying the spatial influence of risk factors and refine risk-based policing interventions.

CHAPTER 5
CCTV VIDEO SURVEILLANCE

RTM Contributions

Video surveillance of public places via closed circuit television (CCTV) cameras has become a common crime prevention tactic over recent decades. Phillips (1999) conducted the first review of closed-circuit television (CCTV) research, documenting evaluations dating as far back as 1978 (Burrows, 1978; Musheno et al., 1978). The time since has seen a dramatic increase in the use of CCTV as a crime prevention tool. By 2002, estimates suggested the presence of over 4.2 million cameras in the UK, a ratio of 1 per every 14 citizens (Norris & McCahill, 2006). Enthusiasm for CCTV spread to the United States, as 49% of local police departments report using CCTV, with usage increasing to 87% for agencies serving jurisdictions with populations of 250,000 or more (Reaves, 2015).

Findings of CCTV research demonstrate the influence of the surrounding environment on CCTV camera effect. The systematic review and meta-analysis of CCTV evaluations conducted by Welsh & Farrington (2009) categorized CCTV interventions across four main settings, with CCTV systems in car parks generating the largest and only statistically significant crime reduction. While a recent update to this review similarly found CCTV to have the largest effect in car parks, CCTV schemes in residential areas were associated with significant crime reductions in certain instances (Piza, Welsh, Farrington, & Thomas, 2019).

While the systematic reviews used overall CCTV systems as the unit of analysis, such a heterogeneous relationship also exists across cameras within individual CCTV systems. In Cincinnati, Lim & Wilcox (2017) found that, while the overall system produced minimal crime control benefits, individual camera sites within residential areas experienced reductions of assault, robbery and burglary with diffusion of benefits being observed much more often than displacement. In Newark, Piza, Caplan, & Kennedy (2014) found that the presence of particular facility types differentially influenced crime occurrence, with bars associated with reductions of violent crime and robbery, retail stores associated with increases in property crime and theft from auto, and schools associated with increased levels of auto theft. Darcan's (2012) analysis of CCTV in Bursa, Turkey used RTM to simultaneously account for multiple spatial risk factors when assessing the interaction between the physical environment and CCTV camera effect. Darcan (2012) began by conducting separate RTM models for 4 crime types: aggravated assault, auto theft, theft from auto, and larceny theft. RTM models included 18 potential environmental risk factors. Darcan (2012) then measured whether the crime prevention effect of CCTV cameras were related to the observed risk score of the surrounding environment. In particular, environmental risk values had a statistically significant, negative relationship with crime for all crime types. This finding demonstrated that CCTV cameras in high-risk areas, as diagnosed via RTM, generated larger crime reductions than CCTV cameras in areas with lower risk values.

Scholars have previously advocated for CCTV deployment to be preceded by an in-depth analysis of the spatial distribution and nature of crime patterns to ensure that cameras are installed in appropriate locations (Ratcliffe, 2006; Welsh & Farrington, 2002). A police agency wishing to combat violent crime, for example, is best served by first identifying specific places experiencing disproportionate levels of violence. Secondly, the specific incidents should be analyzed to identify whether or not the crime activity is susceptible to CCTV. For example, a street corner experiencing a large amount of street-level robberies is a more appropriate camera location than the outside of a mall in which strong-arm robberies occur indoors.

The link between micro-level environmental features and CCTV effects suggests a role for RTM in fine-tuning police-led CCTV interventions by accounting for the composition of the environment when selecting camera sites. Darcan (2012) provides the most straightforward example of how RTM can be a valuable resource in this process. In light of Darcan's findings, jurisdictions can begin their CCTV deployment process by conducting an RTM of their targeted crime types. Then, places exhibiting the highest risk values can be chosen as the final CCTV camera sites. Such a process would help ensure that cameras are placed in a manner that helps maximize their likelihood of success. This process can also be applied to pre-existing CCTV systems to identify specific camera sites to receive additional intervention activities. This is important in light of research finding that the effect of CCTV is heightened when deployed alongside multiple complementary interventions (Piza et al., 2019). In this sense, RTM can help identify cameras that would benefit the most from these types of multi-pronged intervention efforts.

It should also be noted that the RTMDx software can assist with target area selection when individual (rather than cumulative) environmental features are of concern to decision makers. Furthermore, environmental features that may help maximize the effect of CCTV can also be operationalized with RTMDx. This can help account for the types of findings generated in studies such as Lim & Wilcox (2017) and Piza et al. (2014). As an example, let's consider the findings of Piza et al. (2014). Across six separate models, this analysis found that bars were associated with crime reductions while retail stores, schools, and corner stores were associated with crime increases. The implications of these findings for CCTV deployment are simple: cameras should be placed at high crime places, preferably those containing bars and lacking the other identified features, because these areas likely need other intervention mechanisms. GIS shapefiles identifying places falling within the areas of spatial influence for bars, retail stores, schools, and corner stores can be created within RTMDx. Using these disparate GIS layers, analysts can identify the most ideal sites for CCTV cameras: places with high levels of bars and low levels of stores, schools, and corner stores. Then, crimes can be mapped and calculated for each of these potentially ideal sites to select the final locations for CCTV cameras: high crime areas where the environmental composition is most amenable to CCTV camera effect. This process can be adjusted across jurisdictions to account for the spatial risk factors unique to the study setting.

Outside of target selection, RTM can assist in the design of complementary police interventions deployed alongside CCTV. Recent research suggests that the integration of CCTV with proactive police operations is key in maximizing the deterrence effects of video surveillance (Alexandrie, 2017; LaVigne et al., 2011; Piza, Caplan, Kennedy, & Gilchrist, 2015). Piza et al. (2015) conducted an experimental test of this proposition in Newark, NJ. During all experimental tours of duty, one additional CCTV operator was deployed to the control room and exclusively dedicated to monitoring the target areas. In addition, two unmarked patrol units were deployed to the target areas to respond to incidents detected by the experimental operators. Instead of the standard practice of reporting criminal activity through the department's CAD system, the experimental operator reported crime detections directly to the field units via two-way radio. The experiment incorporated a randomized block design with 38 CCTV schemes (encompassing 64 individual cameras) assigned to either the treatment or control group. Piza et al. (2015) found that the experimental strategy generated significant crime prevention benefits in the treatment areas relative to the control areas, with violent crime and disorder significantly reduced during the experimental period. In addition, narcotics activity experienced a statistically significant reduction during the post-experiment period, suggesting the integration of directed patrol and CCTV had a temporally lagged effect on this crime type. These findings are noteworthy, as research has consistently found that stand-alone CCTV systems have had little effect on these types of crime events, particularly violence and disorder (Piza et al., 2019).

The findings of Piza et al. (2015) support the integration of proactive police activity, such as directed patrols, into CCTV operations.[1] However, the findings may

---

[1] While the evaluation of Piza et al. (2015) provides support for this causal mechanism, a quasi-experimental evaluation conducted by (Gerell, 2016) found the implementation of an actively monitored CCTV system, in which CCTV operators directly notified police officers of incidents of concern, did

have some important nuances that future efforts may uncover. In particular, while Piza and colleagues (2015) measured a reduction of crime throughout the entire treatment area, it is possible that certain CCTV locations in the treatment group may have experienced crime declines that were significantly different from other treated areas. This is especially likely in consideration of research finding the effect of Newark's standard CCTV operation differed across camera locations and environmental context, as previously discussed (Piza et al., 2014). Furthermore, recent research suggests that a similar relationship may exist between the physical environment and police actions more generally.

Piza & Gilchrist (2018) used RTM to test whether the high co-location of crime generators and attractors, as measured through RTM, influenced the effect of seven separate police enforcement actions. Interestingly, Piza & Gilchrist (2018) found that, when considered on their own,

---

not reduce assaults in a nightlife area of Malmö, Sweden. It should be noted that Gerell (2016) was not able to measure changes in enforcement levels following the CCTV system, so it is unclear whether the Malmö system incorporated the same causal mechanism as the study of Piza et al. (2015). Nonetheless, the emerging body of work on the merging of proactive police enforcement and CCTV activity suggests that this issue is worthy of additional inquiry from the research community.

a number of police enforcement actions were associated with increased likelihood of crime. Each 1-unit increase in quality of life summonses issued by police, for example, was associated with about an 8% increased likelihood of a shooting. However, when conducted at the places with risk values greater that 2 standard deviations above the mean (i.e. where crime generators and attractors were most concentrated) each 1-unit increase in quality of life summonses was associated with about a 9% decreased likelihood of a shooting. Similar findings were observed for warrant arrests and narcotics arrests. In interpreting these findings, Piza & Gilchrist (2018) argued that *where* officers conduct enforcement actions may be as important as what precise actions they enact.

In considering the findings of Piza & Gilchrist (2018) alongside those of Piza et al. (2014), future replications of the CCTV Directed Patrols experiment can be refined through the use of RTM. For one, researchers can determine whether the effect of police officer patrols were heterogeneous across observed risk levels of the surrounding environment. If such a finding is observed, then directed patrol could be limited to camera sites fitting the ideal environmental context. Furthermore, research such as Piza & Gilchrist (2018) may assist in determining the precise activities that officers should enact during directed patrols. If certain police actions work better in certain areas than others, then these actions can be proactively used only around CCTV sites that fit the environmental context. The scope of this research could also be expanded to include police activities outside of the traditional enforcement actions measured by Piza & Gilchrist (2018). This is important given that risk-based policing interventions have emphasized the use of problem-solving activities in lieu of traditional enforcement (Kennedy et al., 2018).

Contributions to RTM

The emergence of CCTV provides opportunities for the further development of RTM. Leveraging CCTV in such a manner would follow recent research that has used CCTV footage to understand procedural aspects of crime. Levine, Taylor, & Best (2011) used CCTV footage of a city center to measure the influence of group size on the escalation of aggressive behavior to violence while Suonpera, Heinskou & Ejbye-Ernst (2018) measured the risk of injury to bystanders who intervene in violent emergencies. Two studies by Kim Moeller have incorporated CCTV footage of open-air cannabis markets to analyze temporal patterns and trade value of drug transactions (Moeller, 2016, 2017). Researchers have analyzed CCTV footage to better understand the situational dynamics of robbery, including why specific attempts succeed or fail (Nassauer, 2018), the manner by which offenders use different types of weapons to attain dominance (Mosselman et al., 2018), and the threats robbers use to minimize victim resistance (Lindegaard et al., 2018).

Similar research can be used to help uncover the casual mechanisms that may help explain how spatial risk factors increase opportunities for crime. A recent study conducted by Piza & Sytsma (2016) provides an example of these possibilities. Piza & Sytsma (2016) conducted a systematic social observation (SSO) of narcotics transactions captured on CCTV cameras in Newark, NJ. The purpose of the study was to identify the defensive actions drug sellers use to evade detection and apprehension by the police. In certain instances, observations of Piza & Sytsma (2016) clearly noted that the structure of the physical environment played a key role in the drug trade. Stash spots, where drug sellers keep their drug inventory hidden in a proximate location, were commonly used in order to minimize the risk of police discovery of the drug inventory while also allowing quick access when needed. In commercial areas, drug sellers disproportionately made transactions in "public cuts," which are publicly accessible places that have a private dimension by being partially obscured from sight, such as within alleyways or spaces between buildings.

Such analyses moves beyond the identification of environmental features that correlate with crime incidents and begins to explain *how* such features play a role in the criminal process. These findings can be used to develop spatial risk narratives that aid in articulating how the characteristics of high-risk places, as diagnosed via RTM, contribute to the emergence and persistence of crime hot spots (Kennedy et al., 2018). It is also important to note that this methodology can inform risk narratives for a range of crime types besides drug selling. Given that a number of studies have used CCTV footage to study a range of violent crime types (as previously mentioned), this seems like a promising area of research. Rather than focus primarily on human behavior, as SSOs of CCTV footage have primarily done, scholars can focus on the role that environmental features play in the commission of crime.

The SSO of CCTV footage can also help improve risk-based policing efforts by identifying police officer actions that can effectively mitigate risky situations. While not directly focused on this topic, Piza, Caplan, & Kennedy's (2017) SSO of CCTV footage demonstrates this point. Piza et al. (2017) analyzed 9 case studies of serious violent crime incidents captured on CCTV. Piza et al. (2017) did so for the purpose of exploring CCTV's potential as an early intervention strategy that can prevent incidents from escalating to serious violence. The findings supported such a role of CCTV, with the observed violent crime incidents being preceded by 16 unique intervention opportunities, or situations providing legal justification for a police response. However, due to delays in police response commonly caused by the differential response method of police dispatch, CCTV operators only reported 3 of the intervention opportunities. This led Piza et al. (2017) to conclude that the immediate dispatch of officers to intervention opportunities may have prevented the observed serious violent crimes.

The application of Piza et al.'s (2017) methodology to incidents that did not result in violence can help identify police officer actions that could contribute to crime prevention. Each of the 9 incidents included in this study occurred either outside of a bar or public housing complex, two environmental features known to generate crime. Given this fact, it is likely that calls for police service were placed from these locations during the study period. Therefore, a study could have conceptually analyzed police responses to events similar to the intervention opportunities (e.g. drug transactions or disorderly persons) but that did not escalate to violence. Such an analysis could contextualize precisely how police officers mitigated the observed threat. For example, if the response of multiple units or physical separation of involved parties was predominately observed on camera, then these response tactics could be emphasized in risk-based policing interventions. Conversely, if no such patterns were observed, researchers may conclude that conspicuous police presence (rather than any precise actions by the officers) is what should be emphasized during the intervention.

For more information about
risk narratives for risk-based policing, see:

Chapter 3 of *Risk-Based Policing* (ISBN 978-0-520-29563-6)
-or-
www.riskterrainmodeling.com > Topics

CHAPTER 6
POLICE BODY-WORN CAMERAS

RTM Contributions

The last several years have witnessed the emergence of body worn video cameras (BWCs) in policing. The proliferation of BWCs was generated by a number of high-profile use of force incidents, leading the President's Task Force (2015) to identify BWCs as a promising technology to improve police/community relations. Nearly a third of police agencies in the United States report implementing the technology as of 2013 (Reaves, 2015). While similar estimates are not available in other countries, evaluations have been conducted in England (Ellis et al., 2015; Grossmith et al., 2015; Owens, Mann, & McKenna, 2014), Scotland (ODS Consulting, 2011), and Norway (Phelps, Strype, Le Bellu, Lahlou, & Aandal, 2016) suggesting BWC use is international in scope.

In contrast to the systematic reviews conducted on CCTV, BWC reviews have not focused on specific outcome measures, but have rather sought to explore the research questions explored in the literature (Cubitt, Lesic, Myers, & Corry, 2016; Lum, Koper, Merola, Scherer, & Reioux, 2015).

In general, BWC studies have predominately focused on BWC effect on crime (including assault of officers), police officer use of force, and citizen complaints against police (Piza, 2018a). For police in many medium to large jurisdictions, each of these problems may be present simultaneously.

In planning on the deployment of BWCs, monetary costs are an important consideration for police. Startup costs of BWCs represent only a fraction of the total expenditures, and recurring funds must be allocated towards storing recorded video, managing video, providing copies of video to the public upon request, training officers, and administering the program. Additional infrastructure also needs to be purchased, such as docking stations for video upload (Sousa, Coldren, Rodriguez, & Braga, 2016). Costs of the physical BWCs range from $800 to $1,200 per unit, based upon the survey conducted by Miller et al. (2014). These figures pale in comparison to recurring costs, with agencies reporting spending between hundreds of thousands to $2 million per year, with the bulk of expenses going towards data storage costs (Miller et al., 2014). Police departments have listed high costs as a primary reason for not adopting BWCs (Miller et al., 2014) while other agencies have discontinued their BWC programs due to unmanageable expenses (Kindy, 2019).

In the face of monetary constraints, police may opt to deploy BWCs in a piecemeal fashion rather than equip all officers at the outset. In Newark, NJ, for example, the Police Department started issuing BWCs to police officers in a single precinct in June 2017, and continued outfitting officers unit-by-unit until deployment was complete in December 2018 (personal communication with Newark Police Department embedded criminologist Leigh Grossman on 2/25/19). Such a deployment strategy can help an agency mange the expenses associated with project start up while simultaneously identifying technological or organization limitations that may present challenges (Sousa et al., 2016). Despite the practical benefits provided by such an approach, deploying BWCs in such a manner may not provide the most benefit without being preceded by a sufficient problem analysis. Said differently, if the units receiving BWCs first do not stand to gain the most from the technology, piecemeal deployment of BWCs may not achieve maximum efficiency. In this sense, RTM can be used to help prioritize BWC deployment for the purpose of maximizing the likelihood of immediate impact.

Caplan, Marotta, Piza, & Kennedy (2014) conducted an RTM analysis of battery to police officers in Chicago, IL. The final RTM identified 11 spatial risk factors that were significantly related to police battery, with proximity to foreclosed properties exhibiting the largest relative risk value. The composite risk map operationalizing the spatial influence of all 11 risk factors identified cells (i.e., micro places) throughout Chicago that posed the highest risk of police officer battery. The highest risk cells (with risk values greater than 2 standard deviations above the mean) had a 62.53% greater likelihood of experiencing battery compared to police officers managing calls for service at some other locations in Chicago (Caplan et al., 2014: 832).

Given that preventing officer assaults is a key goal of BWC programs, police can use information from RTM to identify priority areas for BWC deployment. To match the units at which officers are deployed, researchers have averaged the risk values of individual cells into an aggregate neighborhood risk of crime (ANROC) value (Drawve, Thomas, & Walker, 2016) for each patrol sector. The ANROC measure was developed for the purpose of aggregating the effect of spatial risk factors up to a neighborhood-level. As such, this measure can be used to identify which specific patrol sectors would most benefit from their officers wearing BWCs.

A jurisdiction interested in adopting BWCs can then run an RTM and aggregate the findings using ANROC for all additional outcomes of interest, such as police use of force and citizen complaints against officers. The result would be the identification of the level to which each sector suffered from assaults against officers, police use of force, and citizen complaints against officers. Conjunctive analysis of case configurations (CACC) (Miethe, Hart, & Regoeczi, 2008), a tool for summarizing categorical data through a matrix of all possible attribute combinations, can then be used to contextualize high-risk outcomes throughout the jurisdiction. A recent study by Connealy & Piza (2019) illustrates this approach. Connealy & Piza (2019) conducted separate RTM analyses for four different robbery types in Denver. Then, they used CACC to identify the cells that were deemed at-risk for multiple robbery types, observing 16 unique combinations of at-risk designation. Interestingly, only about 3% of high-risk places were high-risk for all robbery types, showing how CACC can add important context to RTM by highlighting the precise manner by which high-risk areas co-locate.

The approach of Connealy & Piza (2019) can be similarly used to identify police sectors at-risk of different combinations of BWC-relevant outcomes. Police can first prioritize their program goals and then target the CACC combination that best reflect these aims. For example, if preventing officer assaults is the most desired goal, then police can target all CACC configurations that include the high-risk of officer injuries; agencies most interested in preventing police use of force can target configurations including high-risk of this outcome. If police see preventing officer assaults, police use of force, and citizen complaints as equally important, then patrol sectors with configurations including all of these outcomes can be prioritized. Through such an analysis, police can ensure that the patrol sector most in need of BWCs, in terms of agency priorities, are provided BWCs prior to sectors that have less to benefit from.

Contributions to RTM

The analysis of BWC footage may provide a number of similar benefits as discussed previously in the context of SSO of CCTV footage. Recent studies have begun to leverage BWC footage to analyze encounters between police officers and members of the public. Voigt et al. (2017) analyzed footage from BWCs in Oakland, CA to analyze police interactions with citizens during traffic stops. Through computational linguistic methods, Vogit et al. (2017) measured respectfulness of police officer language towards drivers, finding that officers spoke with consistently less respect towards Blacks as opposed to Whites. Willits & Makin (2018) coded BWC footage from a police department in the Pacific Northwest to determine how long into an incident officers use force and, once force is used, how long it is typically applied. Willits & Makin (2018) found that use of force occurs relatively early in most interactions, but certain variables explain when and how much force is used. For example, officers took more time to apply instrument-based force (e.g. OC spray, bean bags, etc.) and less time to use force against Black suspects.

Given the insights generated by Vogit et al. (2017) and Willits & Makin (2018), researchers may be able to conduct SSOs of BWC to better understand causal mechanisms underlying risk-based policing. For example, the Newark Police Department's risk-based policing intervention involved a police task force visiting businesses in high-risk places and making contact with managers and employees (Kennedy et al., 2018: 87-92). There are a number of different ways that such an activity may generate crime reductions. First, the police officer visits increased police presence within the high-risk area. Given recent research demonstrating the effect of increased police presence in high-crime places (Nagin & Weisburd, 2013; Nagin, Solow, & Lum, 2015), this may help explain the nature of the crime reduction. Conversely, by speaking with business managers and employees, police officers may gain intelligence on the nature of crime in the surrounding area. The systematic analysis of BWC footage may help police analysts identify which of these two mechanisms is most responsible for observed crime reductions. This information may be used to inform the nature of directed patrols, specifically in terms of whether any specific micro-places (e.g. a certain street corner) deserve more attention or if any particular situations (e.g. patrons exiting a bar alone) create a heighted risk of a violent attack.

Coupled with CCTV footage, SSOs of BWC can also shed light on effective police actions taken during risk-based policing interventions. As previously discussed, the analysis of CCTV footage would allow researchers to observe general patterns in police response and physical behavior. BWC footage provides more granular insight through a ground-level view and audio capturing officer communication with those on scene. This can help provide more detailed insight on the nature of police activity. As an example, the Glendale Police Department's risk-based policing intervention relied on patrol officers distributing flyers to citizens to inform them of the robbery risk associated with brandishing their electronics on the street. BWC footage could help garner important insight on this activity. For example, researchers can identify whether these police/citizen interactions were limited to the distribution of flyers, or if the police officer provided further verbal explanation to the citizen. Similar to as in Newark, researchers can also determine if Glendale Police Officers received any helpful intelligence from citizens during such exchanges. Researchers can also use BWC footage to diagnose citizen responses to receiving a flyer, particularly if they seem to welcome such interactions with police. Such information can be used in the development of future risk-based policing efforts. This is especially the case when considering likely future iterations of BWCs.

Police agencies have begun utilizing wearable GPS devices to track the location of officers during foot patrol activities (Ariel & Partridge, 2017; Wain, Ariel, & Tankebe, 2017). Given the rapid advancement of BWC technologies, with advanced systems now including biometric monitoring sensors and WiFi mesh network connectivity (Siberglitt, Lauland, Watson, Eusebi, & Lastunen, 2017), GPS tracking may soon be standard in BWCs. This location information could be combined with the aforementioned qualitative findings to uncover contextual aspects of risk-based policing activities. For example, GPS-enabled BWC data would allow researchers to determine if citizen receptivity or citizen-generated intelligence varied across levels of concentration (Piza & Gilchrist, 2018) or unique configurations (Caplan, Kennedy, Barnum, & Piza, 2017) of spatial risk factors. And, it would enable assessments of how officer behaviors, and their own personal risk perceptions, vary by geographic settings.

CHAPTER 7
GUNSHOT DETECTION SYSTEMS

RTM Contributions

Gunshot Detection Systems (GDS) incorporate networks of acoustic sensors that detect and identify the location of gunfire events in real time. GDS implementation by police has become popular in the US. While only 4% of police agencies in the US overall use the technology, larger agencies much more often report investments in GDS. 50%, 30%, and 28% of jurisdictions with at least 1 million, 500,000, and 250,000 residents, respectively, use GDS according to the most recent estimates (Reaves, 2015).

According to descriptions from research on GDS (e.g. Carr & Doleac, 2016; Irvin-Erickson, La Vigne, Levine, Tiry, & Bieler, 2017; Mares & Blackburn, 2012; Watkins, Mazerolle, Rogan, & Frank, 2002) police tend to install GDS sensors across large, contiguous areas of the jurisdiction. It is fair to consider whether this is a cost-effective deployment of the technology. This is especially the case in light of the monetary cost associated with GDS. According to the website of ShotSpotter, the industry leader in GDS, subscriptions of the technology cost between $65,000 and

$90,000 per square mile per year. Therefore, installing GDS across a large contiguous area may not be a cost-effective strategy. As discussed earlier, crime-and-place research shows crime to be highly concentrated with a very small number of micro-places accounting for the majority of crime events (Lee et al., 2017). Therefore, contiguous deployment of GDS sensors may cover a large number of places at low risk of shooting events.

A recent field experiment by Ratcliffe, Lattanzio, Kikuchi, & Thomas (2019) suggests that contiguous deployment of GDS can be replaced with a method that better reflects the clustered distribution of crime. In this study, the Philadelphia Police Department installed 17 acoustic GDS sensors at pre-existing CCTV camera locations spread throughout high-crime places in the city. This approach seems to better target gunfire events than the deployment of GDS over large, contiguous geographies.

In light of the potential for targeting micro-level hot spots with GDS, the question becomes how police can go about selecting places to receive the acoustic sensors. Hot spot mapping techniques have long been the standard method for selecting micro-places for geographically focused police interventions. However, a body of research has emerged demonstrating that RTM can improve upon the predictive accuracy of forecasts conducted via hot spot techniques. Caplan et al. (2011), the inaugural RTM analysis, demonstrated that forecasts of shooting incidents in Irvington, NJ conducted with RTM were more accurate across two 6-month time periods than retrospective hot spot mapping. Kennedy et al.'s (2011) replication of Caplan et al. (2011) in Newark, NJ provided similar support, with RTM forecasts outperforming hot spot maps over four 4-month time periods. Recent research has found that combing RTM with other event-dependent methods further improves place-based forecasts. Caplan et al. (2019) compared the predictive accuracy of RTM, kernel density (KDE) hot spot mapping, and a hybrid model integrating both techniques for street robbery in Brooklyn, NY. They found that over both 1-month and 3-month intervals, the integrated technique outperformed both the RTM-only and KDE-only models. Garnier et al. (2018) conducted a similar analysis of robbery in Newark, NJ, substituting the KDE approach for spatiotemporal "near repeat" analysis. Similar to Caplan et al. (2019), Garnier et al. (2018) found through simulation modeling that integrating both techniques (RTM and spatiotemporal event-dependent) outperformed both the RTM-only and spatiotemporal-only models. In short, this body of research shows that RTM can help maximize the effect of GDS by identifying the micro-places most at-risk of future shooting events as optimal target areas. This would have the additional benefit of allowing for less expensive deployment of GDS while still achieving optimal impact.

RTM may also help overcome what recent research suggests may be a limitation of GDS, potential false positive gunfire events detected by the acoustic sensors. Litch and Orrison (2011) explicitly measured whether physical evidence of a gunshot was found on the scene of events detected by GDS. Their analysis found that 58% and 33% of GDS dispatches were determined to be "false alarms" in Hampton and Newport News, respectively (see Litch & Orrison, 2011, Table 8: p. 40). The analysis of Ratcliffe et al. (2019) determined that unfounded shootings (i.e. officers finding no on-scene evidence to confirm a gunfire event occurred) significantly increased 259% in target areas as compared to control areas following the deployment of GDS. While Ratcliffe et al. (2019) acknowledged that a case being classified as unfounded does not automatically mean a gunshot event did not occur (as officers may not successfully locate evidence in all cases), the rather large increase in unfounded events demonstrates that false positive events generated by GDS warrant further attention from the research community.

Similar to how RTM can be used to identify target areas for GDS sensors, it may also be used to identify areas where the installation of acoustic sensors should be avoided. This is especially the case when police are considering the expansion of existing GDS coverage areas. In this sense, researchers can conduct an RTM on all unfounded shootings detected by GDS, which could be considered as false positive detections. The findings of these models would identify the environmental settings most at risk of false positive GDS detections, with these places being eliminated from GDS target area consideration.

Contributions to RTM

While acknowledging the aforementioned issues of potential false positives (Litch & Orrison, 2011; Ratcliffe et al., 2019), research on GDS finds that the technology can significantly increase the proportion of gunfire events that come to the attention of the police. Given that official data sources largely rely on citizens reporting crime to the police, selective underreporting can introduce bias into common measures of gunfire events. This may be especially problematic in high-violence, disenfranchised neighborhoods where police may not possess the perceived legitimacy necessary for residents to trust that a police response would be helpful (Kirk & Matsuda, 2011).

Carr and Doleac (2016) leveraged data from Washington, DC and Oakland, CA over two different temporal periods and employed panel regression models to determine the correlation between GDS detections and citizen reports of shots fired, homicides, and assault with a deadly weapon within hourly periods. The findings suggest that only about 12% of gunfire events resulted in a 9-1-1 call to report gunshots and only 2-7% resulted in a report of assault with a deadly weapon. Irvin-Erickson *et al.* (2017) also used data from Washington, DC to calculate the relative sensitivity of GDS: the ratio of GDS detections to calls for service. Within the 20-minute window from GDS alerts (the default time frame used in the analysis), they found a relative GDS sensitivity of 1.52. Their findings also showed that GDS sensitivity significantly varied by month, day of the year, weekends vs. weekdays, and hour of the day. However, in most cases GDS-to-calls ratios were above 1, supporting the general notion that GDS accurately detects gunfire events. An earlier study by Litch and Orrison (2011) refined the comparison of GDS and 9-1-1 calls by incorporating data about the on-scene evidence associated with gunfire events. In their overall sample, Litch & Orrison, (2011) found that only 18% of GDS alerts had an associated 9-1-1 call in Hampton, VA, suggesting that 85% of gunfire incidents would not have been detected absent GDS. When restricting their analysis to incidents with physical evidence of a gunshot, only 39% of "confirmed" gunfire incidents had an associated 9-1-1 call. While lower than the previous figure, this still suggests that a majority of gunfire events (61%) would not have been detected without GDS. Litch and Orrison (2011) found similar results for Newport News: only 24% of GDS detections and 43% of "confirmed" detections had associated 9-1-1 calls.

In light of these findings, spatial analyses of gunfire events relying solely on police records may be incomplete. As such, GDS data can provide researchers with the totality of gunfire events that occurred within a city, which may improve upon the face validity of the analysis. A number of near repeat studies have begun to incorporate GDS data. Mazeika & Uriarte (2018) demonstrated the potential value of GDS data in their analysis of gun violence in Trenton, NJ. In short, the inclusion of GDS data refined the findings of the near repeat analysis. Findings incorporating the GDS data identified smaller geographic areas of near-repeat clusters and generated more frequent near repeat chains than findings based only on police reported data. As such, the GDS data helped to refine the identification of spatiotemporal gun violence clusters. It is possible that the inclusion of GDS into RTM research can have a similar benefit over using only police reported data.

CHAPTER 8
CONCLUSION

This report outlined a number of benefits that RTM can offer to a range of contemporary police technologies, including CCTV, BWC, and GDS. Conversely, information gathered from many of these technologies can improve upon RTM analysis products as well as risk-based policing efforts. As such, the integration of RTM with these police technologies can generate benefits for both research and practice, as well as attempts to better integrate these complementary, but too often divided, aspects of evidence-based policing.

Modern police agencies can manage these technology integration efforts through a number of organizational units and processes. The last few decades has seen the emergence of research and planning units in police organizations (Bond & Gabriele, 2018). Research and planning units have traditionally performed a number of functions for police, including researching best practices, conducting needs assessment, and developing policy, to name a few (Haberman & King, 2011). These units can help support evidence-based practices. Police departments with formal research and planning units report significantly greater levels of innovative practices than those without these units (Bond & Gabriele, 2018). In this sense, research and planning units can help identify opportunities from RTM-technology integrations across a range of both existing and forthcoming technology deployments. These units can also draft policies to guide these integration efforts and promote best practices in their use.

Police can monitor the implementation and ongoing effect of RTM-technology integrations though standard law enforcement management strategies. CompStat meetings are perhaps the most common of these approaches, with police agencies around the United States adopting CompStat for the purpose of measuring police performance (Bratton & Malinowski, 2008; Weisburd, Mastrofski, McNally, Greenspan, & Willis, 2003; Willis, Mastrofski, & Weisburd, 2007). Other performance management strategies have emerged recently, such as crime analysis meetings meant to support the Stratified Model of policing (Santos, 2013) and, as previously discussed, ACTION meetings meant to support Risk-based policing (Caplan & Kennedy, 2016; Kennedy et al., 2018). Through each of these approaches, police can communicate the purpose of

RTM-technology integrations to police commanders, track the progress of program implementation across divisions, continuously measure whether the programs are having the intended effect, and adjust strategy as needed to help ensure that maximum benefit is achieved.

Given the relation RTM has with multiple technologies, it is possible for a police agency to simultaneously deploy a number of these integration efforts. Given the amount of data that is collected and generated by these systems, crime analysts may generate more temporally and spatially precise insights on emerging crime patterns than what is possible outside such a data-rich environment. This process may present challenges to traditional police oversight processes. For example, Haberman & Ratcliffe (2012) noted that the typical weekly or bi-weekly schedule of police performance meetings does not provide police commanders adequate opportunity to respond to crime patterns that may subside within that time frame. While Haberman & Ratcliffe (2012) made this observation in regards to CompStat meetings, such an issue would seem to apply to any meeting-based approach to program oversight. In this sense, the emergence of Real-Time Crime Centers may help foster the integration of RTM with other police technologies. Real-Time Crime Centers provide police with an integrated solution for analyzing large amounts of data for the purpose of improving situational awareness (Fox, 2014). As these centers become more ingrained into daily police functions, agencies may be better positioned to proactively manage RTM-technology integrations.

This report also points to the importance of designing evaluation studies to determine the effect of RTM-technology integrations. In considering such efforts, the literature is encouraging, as the technologies discussed in this report have consistently been subjected to rigorous case-controlled evaluations. BWC evaluations, in particular, have been rigorously studied, with a larger proportion of evaluations incorporating randomized-controlled trial designs for BWCs than other crime control technologies (Piza, 2018a). Randomization is not as commonplace in the CCTV literature, but random experiments have been conducted (Hayes & Downs, 2011; La Vigne & Lowry, 2011; Piza et al., 2015). When randomization has not been possible, a number of researchers have used statistical matching techniques to maximize interval validity (Farrington, Gill, Waples, & Argomaniz, 2007; Piza, 2018b) or leveraged naturally occurring social occurrences to reduce endogeneity, when the allocation of CCTV is correlated with unobserved factors that determine crime (Alexandrie, 2017). While research on GDS is the least developed of the technologies included in this report, the partially randomized field experiment conducted by Ratcliffe et al. (2019) suggests that sophisticated research methods can be applied to this technology as well. In sum, establishing a robust research portfolio around the integration of RTM with CCTV, BWC, and GDS seems highly possible. Such research would present opportunities for tests of the effect of RTM-technology integrations as well as the generation of information that can support the further development of RTM and Risk-Based Policing.

For more information about
RTM and Risk-Based Policing, see:

www.riskterrainmodeling.com
-and-
www.riskbasedpolicing.com

Read more about some of the research studies mentioned in
this report at the **Rutgers Center on Public Security**, where
you'll find downloadable briefs and full-text articles:

www.rutgerscps.org

REFERENCES

Alexandrie, G. (2017). Surveillance cameras and crime : a review of randomized and natural experiments natural experiments. *Journal of Scandinavian Studies in Criminology and Crime Prevention, 18*(2), 210–222.

Ariel, B., & Partridge, H. (2017). Predictable Policing: Measuring the Crime Control Benefits of Hotspots Policing at Bus Stops. *Journal of Quantitative Criminology, 33*(4), 809–833.

Bayley, D. H. (1994). *Police for the future.* New York: Oxford University Press.

Berman, G. and Fox, A. (2010). *Trial & Error in Criminal Justice Reform. Learning From Failure.* Washington, DC: Urban Institute Press.

Bond, B. J., & Gabriele, K. R. (2018). Research and planning units: An innovation instrument in the 21st-century police organization. *Criminal Justice Policy Review, 29*(1), 67–88.

Braga, A. A., Papachristos, A. V., & Hureau, D. M. (2014). The Effects of Hot Spots Policing on Crime: An Updated Systematic Review and Meta-Analysis. *Justice Quarterly, 31*(4), 633–663.

Brantingham, P. L. & Brantingham, P. J. (1993). Environment, routine and situation: Toward a pattern theory of crime. In Ronald Clarke and Marcus Felson (eds.), *Routine Activity and Rational Choice, Advances in Criminological Theory* (vol. 5, pp. 259-294). New Brunswick, NJ: Transaction Publishers.

Bratton, W. J., & Malinowski, S. W. (2008). Police Performance Management in Practice: Taking COMPSTAT to the Next Level. *Policing, 2*(3), 259–265.

Caplan, J. M. (2011). Mapping the Spatial Influence of Crime Correlates: A Comparison of Operationalization Schemes and Implications for Crime Analysis and Criminal Justice Practice. *Cityscape: A Journal of Policy Development and Research @BULLET, 13*(3), 57–83.

Caplan, J. M. & Kennedy, L. W. (2013). Risk terrain modeling diagnsotics utility (version 1.0). Newark, NJ: Rutgers Center on Public Security.

Caplan, J. M. & Kennedy, L. W. (2016). *Risk terrain modeling. Crime prediction and risk reduction.* Oakland, CA: University of California Press.

Caplan, J., Kennedy, L., Piza, E., & Barnum, J. (2019). Using Vulnerability and Exposure to Improve Robbery Prediction and Target Area Selection. *Applied Spatial Analysis and Policy,* DOI: 10.1007/s12061-019-09294-7.

75

Caplan, J. M., Kennedy, L. W., Barnum, J. D., & Piza, E. L. (2017). Crime in Context: Utilizing Risk Terrain Modeling and Conjunctive Analysis of Case Configurations to Explore the Dynamics of Criminogenic Behavior Settings. *Journal of Contemporary Criminal Justice, 33*(2), 133–151.

Caplan, J. M., Kennedy, L. W., & Miller, J. (2011). Risk Terrain Modeling : Brokering Criminological Theory and GIS Methods for Crime Forecasting Risk Terrain Modeling : Brokering Criminological Theory and GIS Methods for Crime Forecasting. *Justice Quarterly, 28*(2), 360–381.

Caplan, J. M., Marotta, P., Piza, E. L., & Kennedy, L. W. (2014). Spatial risk factors of felonious battery to police officers. *Policing : An International Journal of Police Strategies & Management, 37*(4), 823–838.

Carr, J. B., & Doleac, J. L. (2016). The geography, incidence, and underreporting of gun violence: new evidence using ShotSpotter data. *Available at SSRN.* http://doi.org/10.2139/ssrn.2770506

Clarke, R. V, & Eck, J. E. (2005). *Crime Analysis for Problem Solvers in 60 Small Steps.* Washington, D.C.

Connealy, N. T., & Piza, E. L. (2019). Risk factor and high-risk place variations across different robbery targets in Denver, Colorado. *Journal of Criminal Justice, 60*, 47–56.

Cubitt, T. I., Lesic, R., Myers, G. L., & Corry, R. (2016). Body-worn video: A systematic review of literature. *Australian & New Zealand Journal of Criminology*, 1–18.

Darcan, E. (2012). *The impact of police-monitored CCTV cameras on crime patterns: A quasi-experimental study in the metropolitan city of Bursa, Turkey.* Doctoral dissertation, University of Rutgers, NJ.

Drawve, G., Thomas, S. A., & Walker, J. T. (2016). Bringing the physical environment back into neighborhood research: The utility of RTM for developing an aggregate neighborhood risk of crime measure. *Journal of Criminal Justice, 44*, 21–29.

Eck, J. E. (2006). When is a bologna sandwich better than sex ? A defense of small-n case study evaluations. *Journal of Experimental Criminology, 2*(3), 345–362.

Ellis, T., Jenkins, T. and Smith, P. (2015). *Evaluation of the introduction of personal issue body worn video cameras (Operation Hyperion) on the Isle of Wright.* Final Report to Hampshire Constabulary. University of Portsmouth: Institute of Criminal Justice Studies.

Farrington, D., Gottfredson, D., Sherman, L. & Welsh, B. (2002). The Maryland Scientific Methods Scale. In Sherman, L., Farrington, D.,

Welsh, B., & MacKenzie, D. (eds.). *Evidence-Based Crime Prevention. Revised Edition*: 13-21. New York: Routledge.

Farrington, D. P., Gill, M., Waples, S. J., & Argomaniz, J. (2007). The effects of closed-circuit television on crime: Meta-analysis of an English national quasi-experimental multi-site evaluation. *Journal of Experimental Criminology*, *3*(1), 21–38.

Ferguson, A. G. (2017). *The rise of big data policing. Surveillance, race, and the future of law enforcement.* New York: New York University Press.

Fox, M. (2014, April 15). *How real-time crime center technologies are force multipliers. New technologies promise to connect disparate systems for improved situational awareness.* PoliceOne.com. Retrieved 4/9/19 from https://www.policeone.com/police-products/police-technology/articles/7083433-How-real-time-crime-center-technologies-are-force-multipliers/.

Gaines, L. & Kappeler, V. (2005). *Policing in America. Fifth Edition.* New York: Lexis Nexus, Anderson Publishing.

Garnier, S., Caplan, J. M., & Kennedy, L. W. (2018). Predicting Dynamical Crime Distribution From Environmental and Social Influences. *Frontiers in Applied Mathematics and Statistics*, *4*(13), 1–10.

Gerell, M. (2016). Hot Spot Policing With Actively Monitored CCTV Cameras: Does it Reduce Assaults in Public Places? *International Criminal Justice Review*, *26*(2), 187–201.

Gerell, M. (2018). Bus Stops and Violence, Are Risky Places Really Risky? *European Journal on Criminal Policy and Research*, (April), 1–21.

Gottfredson, M. & Hirschi, T. (1990). *A general theory of crime.* Stanford: Stanford University Press.

Greene, J. R. (2014). New Directions in Policing: Balancing Prediction and Meaning in Police Research. *Justice Quarterly*, *31*(2), 193–228.

Grossmith, L., Owens, C., Finn, W., Mann, D., Davies, T., & Baika, L. (2015). *Police, cameras, evidence: London's cluster randomised controlled trial of body worn video.* London, England: College of Policing.

Haberman, C. P. (2017). Overlapping hot spots? Examination of spatial heterogeneity of hot spots of different criem types. *Criminology & Public Policy*, *16*(2), 633–660.

Haberman, C. P. & King, W. R. (2011). The role of research and planning units in law enforcement organizations. *Policing: An International Journal of Police Strategies & Management, 34*, 687-698.

Haberman, C. P. & Ratcliffe, J. H. (2012). The Predictive Policing Challenges of Near Repeat Armed Street Robberies. *Policing*, *6*(2), 151–166.

Hayes, R., & Downs, D. M. (2011). Controlling retail theft with CCTV domes, CCTV public view monitors, and protective containers: A randomized controlled trial. *Security Journal*, *24*, 237–250.

Irvin-Erickson, Y., La Vigne, N., Levine, N., Tiry, E., & Bieler, S. (2017). What does Gunshot Detection Technology tell us about gun violence? *Applied Geography*, *86*, 262–273.

Kelling, G., Pate, T., Dieckman, D., & Brown, C. (1974). *The Kansas City Prventative Patro Experiment.* Washington, DC: The Police Foundation.

Kennedy, L. W., Caplan, J. M., & Piza, E. (2011). Risk Clusters, Hotspots, and Spatial Intelligence: Risk Terrain Modeling as an Algorithm for Police Resource Allocation Strategies. *Journal of Quantitative Criminology*, *27*(3), 339–362.

Kennedy, L. W., Caplan, J. M., & Piza, E. L. (2018). *Risk-Based Policing: Evidence-Based Crime Prevention with Big Data and Spatial Analytics.* Oakland, CA: University of California Press.

Kennedy, L. W., Caplan, J. M., Piza, E. L., & Buccine-Schraeder, H. (2016). Vulnerability and exposure to crime: Applying risk terrain modeling to the study of assault in Chicago. *Applied Spatial Analysis and Policy*, *9*(4), 529–548.

Kindy, K. (2019, January 21). *Some U.S. police departments dump body-camera programs amid high costs.* Washington Post. Retreived 3/6/19 from https://www.washingtonpost.com/national/some-us-police-departments-dump-body-camera-programs-amid-high-costs/2019/01/21/991f0e66-03ad-11e9-b6a9-0aa5c2fcc9e4_story.html?utm_term=.698813e5947e.

Kirk, D. S., & Matsuda, M. (2011). Legal Cynicism, Collective Efficacy, And The Ecology Of Arrest. *Criminology*, *49*(2), 443–472.

Klockars, C. (e.d.). (1983). *Thining about police.* New York: McGraw-Hill.

La Vigne, N. & Lowry, S. (2011). *Evaluation of camera use to prevent crime in commuter parking facilities: a randomized controlled trial. Technical Report of The Urban Institute Justice Policy Center* (Vol. 1). Washington, D.C.: Urban Institute.

LaVigne, N. G., Lowry, S. S., Markman, J. A., & Dwyer, A. M. (2011). *Evaluating the Use of Public Surveillance Cameras for Crime Control and Prevention.* Washington, D.C.: Urban Institute..

Lee, Y., Eck, J. E., O, S., & Martinez, N. N. (2017). How concentrated is crime at places ? A systematic review from 1970 to 2015. *Crime Science.*

Levine, M., Taylor, P. and Best, R. (2011). Third parties, violence, and conflict resolution: The role of group size and collective action in the microregulation of violence. *Psychological Science, 22*(3), 406-412.

Lim, H., & Wilcox, P. (2017). Crime-reduction effects of open-street CCTV: Conditionality considerations. *Justice Quarterly, 34*(4), 597–626.

Litch, M., & Orrison, G. A. (2011). For SECURES Demonstration in Hampton and Newport News , Virginia Configuration Item Number : 13xxx-1xx.

Lindegaard, M., de Vries, T., & Bernasco, W. (2018). Patterns of force, sequences of resistance: Revisiting luckenbill with robberies caught on camera. *Deviant Behavior,* DOI: 10.1080/01639625.2017.1407100.

Lum, C., Koper, C., Merola, L., Scherer, A., & Reioux, A. (2015). *Existing and Ongoing Body Worn Camera Research: Knowledge Gaps and Opportunities. Report for the Laura and John Arnold Foundation. Fairfax, VA: Center for Evidence-Based Crime Policy, George Mason University.*

Lum, C., Koper, C. S., & Telep, C. W. (2011). The Evidence-Based Policing Matrix. *Journal of Experimental Criminology, 7*(1), 3–26.

Lum, C., and Koper, C. (2017). *Evidence-Based Policing: Translating Research into Practice.* Oxford, UK: Oxford University Press.

Lum, C., Koper, C. S., & Willis, J. (2017). Understanding the Limits of Technology's Impact on Police Effectiveness. *Police Quarterly, 20*(2), 135–163.

Manning, P. (2008). *The Technology of Policing: Crime Mapping, Information Technology, and the Rationality of Crime Control.* New York: New York University Press.

Mares, D., & Blackburn, E. (2012). Evaluating the Effectiveness of an Acoustic Gunshot Location System in St. Louis, MO. *Policing, 6*(1), 26–42.

Mastrofki, S. and Willis, J. (2011). Police Organization. In Tonry, M. (ed.) *The Oxford Handbook of Crime and Criminal Justice.* pp. 479-508. Oxford University Press: Oxford, UK.

Mazeika, D. M., & Uriarte, L. (2018). The near repeats of gun violence using acoustic triangulation data. *Security Journal.*

Miller, W. (1977). *Cops and bobbies: Police authority in New York and London, 1830-1870.* Chicago: University of Chicago Press.

Miller, T., Toliver, J., & Police Executive Research Forum (PERF). (2014). *Implementing a body-worn camera program: Recomendations and lessons learned.* Washington, DC: U.S. Department of Justice, Community Oriented Policing Services.

Moeller, K. (2016). Temporal transaction patterns in an open-air cannabis market. *Police Practice and Research, 17*(1), 37-50.

Moeller, K. (2017). Video-recorded retail cannabis trades in a low-risk marketplace: Trade value and temporal patterns. *Journal of Research in Crime and Delinquency,* 1–22.

Mosselman, F., Weenink, D., & Lindegaard, M. (2018). Weapons, body postures, and the quest for dominance in robberies. *Journal of Research in Crime and Delinquency,* 55(1): 3-26.

Nagin, D., Solow, R., and Lum, C. (2015). Deterrence, criminal opportunities, and police. *Criminology, 53*(1): 74-100.

Nagin, D. and Weisburd, D. (2013). Evidence and public policy. The example of evaluation research in policing. *Criminology & Public Policy, 12*(4): 651-679.

Nassauer, A. (2018). How robberies succeed or fail. *Journal of Research in Crime and Delinquency,* 55(1): 125-154.

Norris, C., & Armstrong, G. (1999). CCTV and the Social Structuring of Surveillance. *Surveillance of Public Space, 10,* 157–178.

Norris, C., & McCahill, M. (2006). CCTV: Beyond penal modernism? *British Journal of Criminology, 46*(1), 97–118.

ODS Consulting. (2011). *Body worn video projects in Paisley and Aberdeen, self evaluation.* Glasgow: ODS Consulting.

Owens, C., Mann, D., & McKenna, R. (2014). *The Essex body worn video trial: The impact of body worn video on criminal justice outcomes of domestic abuse incidents.* London, England: College of Policing.

Perry, W. L., McInnes, B., Price, C. C., Smith, S. C., & Hollywood, J. S. (2013). *Predictive Policing: The Role of Crime Forecasting in Law Enforcement Operations.* Santa Monica, CA.: RAND Corporation.

Phelps, J. M., Strype, J., Le Bellu, S., Lahlou, S., & Aandal, J. (2016). Experiential learning and simulation-based training in Norwegian police education: examining body-worn video as a tool to encourage reflection. *Policing,* 1–16.

Phillips, C. (1999). A review of CCTV evaluations: Crime reduction effects and attitudes towards its use. *Crime Prevention Studies, 10,* 123–155.

Piza, E. L. (2018a). The history, policy implications, and knowledge gaps of the CCTV literature: Insights for the development of body-worn video camera research. *International Criminal Justice Review*, DOI: 10.1177/1057567718759583.

Piza, E. L. (2018). The crime prevention effect of CCTV in public places: A propensity score analysis. *Journal of Crime and Justice*, *41*(1), 14-30.

Piza, E. L., Caplan, J. M., & Kennedy, L. W. (2014). Analyzing the influence of micro-level factors on CCTV camera effect. *Journal of Quantitative Criminology*, *30*(2), 237–264.

Piza, E. L., Caplan, J. M., & Kennedy, L. W. (2017). CCTV as a tool for early police intervention: Preliminary lessons from nine case studies. *Security Journal*, *30*(1), 247–265.

Piza, E. L., Caplan, J. M., Kennedy, L. W., & Gilchrist, A. M. (2015). The effects of merging proactive CCTV monitoring with directed police patrol: A randomized controlled trial. *Journal of Experimental Criminology*, *11*(1), 43–69.

Piza, E. L., Feng, S., Kennedy, L., & Caplan, J. (2017). Place-based correlates of motor vehicle theft and recovery: Measuring spatial influence across neighbourhood context. *Urban Studies*, *54*(13), 2998–3021.

Piza, E. L., & Feng, S. Q. (2017). The Current and Potential Role of Crime Analysts in Evaluations of Police Interventions : Results From a Survey of the International Association of Crime Analysts. *Police Quarterly*, 1–28.

Piza, E. L., & Gilchrist, A. M. (2018). Measuring the effect heterogeneity of police enforcement actions across spatial contexts. *Journal of Criminal Justice*, *54*, 76–87.

Piza, E. L., Kennedy, L. W., & Caplan, J. M. (2018). Facilitators and impediments to designing, implementing, and evaluating risk-based policing strategies using risk terrain modeling : Insights from a multi-city evaluation in the United States. *European Journal on Criminal Policy and Research*, *24*(4), 489–513.

Piza, E. L., & Sytsma, V. A. (2016). Exploring the defensive actions of drug sellers in open-air markets: A systematic social observation. *Journal of Research in Crime and Delinquency*, *53*(1), 36–65.

Piza, E. L., Welsh, B. C., Farrington, D. P., & Thomas, A. L. (2019). CCTV surveillance for crime prevention. A 40-year systematic review with meta-analysis. *Criminology & Public Policy*, *18*(1), 135–139.

President's Task Force on 21st Century Policing (2015). *Final report of the President's Task Force on 21st Century Policing.* Washington, DC: Office of Community Oriented Policing Services.

Ratcliffe, J. (2006). *Video Surveillance of Public Places.* Problem-Oriented Guides for Police. Response Guide Series. Guide No. 4. Washington, DC: U.S. Department of Justice, Office of Community Oriented Policing Services, Center for Problem-Oriented Policing.

Ratcliffe, J. H., Lattanzio, M., Kikuchi, G., & Thomas, K. (2019). A partially randomized field experiment on the effect of an acoustic gunshot detection system on police incident reports. *Journal of Experimental Criminology*, *15*(1), 67–76.

Salvemini, A. V., Piza, E. L., Carter, J. G., Grommon, E. L., & Merritt, N. (2015). Integrating human factors engineering and information processing approaches to facilitate evaluations in criminal justice technology research. *Evaluation Review*, *39*(3), 308–338.

Sampson, R. J., Winship, C., & Knight, C. (2013). Translating causal claims: Principles and strategies for policy-relevant criminology. *Criminology & Public Policy*, *12*(4), 587–616.

Santos, R. B. (2013). Implementation of a police organizational model for crime reduction. *Policing: An International Journal of Police Strategies & Management*, *36*(2), 295–311.

Santos, R. B. (2014). The Effectiveness of Crime Analysis for Crime Reduction : Cure or Diagnosis ? *Journal of Contemporary Criminal Justice*, *30*(2), 147–168.

Sherman, L. (2011). Police and Crime Control. In Tonry, M. (ed.) *The Oxford Handbook of Crime and Criminal Justice.* pp. 509-537. Oxford University Press: Oxford, UK.

Sherman, L. W. (1998). Ideas in American Policing Evidence-Based Policing. *Ideas in American Policing Evidence-Based Policing.*

Sherman, L. W., Gartin, P. R., & Buerger, M. E. (1989). Hot spots of predatory crime: Routine activites and the criminology of place. *Criminology*, *27*(1), 27–55.

Sherman, L. W., & Weisburd, D. (1995). General deterrent effects of police patrol in crime "hot spots": A randomized , controlled trial. *Justice Quarterly*, *12*(4), 625–648.

Silberglitt, R., Lauland, A., Watson, M., Eusebi, S., & Lastunen, J. (2017). *Wearable technologies for law enforcement. Multifunctional vest system options.* Priority Criminal Justice Needs Initiative. RAND Corporation: Santa Monica, CA.

Skogan, W. & Frydl, K. (2004). *Fairness and effectivenss in policing: The evidence.* Committee to review research on police policy and practices. Committee on law and justice, divison of behavioral and social sciences and education. Washington, DC: The National Academies Press.

Sousa, W. H., Coldren, J. R. J., Rodriguez, D., & Braga, A. A. (2016). Research on Body Worn Cameras: Meeting the Challenges of Police Operations, Program Implementation, and Randomized Controlled Trial Designs. *Police Quarterly*, *19*(3), 363–384.

Sparrow, M. K. (2011). *Governing science. New perspectives in policing. Executive session on policing and public safety.* Washington, DC: U.S. Department of Justice, Office of Justice Programs, National Institute of Justice.

Suonpera, L., Heinskou, M., and Ejbye-Ernst, P. (2018). On the actual risk of bystander interventions: A statistical study based on naturally occurring violent emergencies. *Journal of Research in Crime and Delinquency*, *55*(1), 27-50.

Voigt, R., Camp, N. P., Prabhakaran, V., Hamilton, W. L., Hetey, R. C., Griffiths, C. M., ... Eberhardt, J. L. (2017). Language from police body camera footage shows racial disparities in officer respect. *Proceedings of the National Academy of Sciences of the United States of America*, *114*(25), 6521–6526.

Wain, N., Ariel, B., & Tankebe, J. (2017). The collateral consequences of GPS-LED supervision in hot spots policing. *Police Practice and Research*, *4263*(April), 1–15.

Watkins, C., Mazerolle, L. G., Rogan, D., & Frank, J. (2002). Technological Approaches to Controlling Random Gunfire. Results of a GunShot Detection System Field Test. *Policing: An International Journal of Police Strategies & Management*, *25*(2), 345–370.

Weisburd, D., Braga, A. A., Groff, E. R., & Wooditch, A. (2017). Can hot spots policing reduce crime in urban areas? An agent-based simulation. *Criminology*, *55*(1), 137–173.

Weisburd, D., & Eck, J. E. (2004). What Can Police Do to Reduce Crime, Disorder, and Fear? *The Annals of the American Academy of Political and Social Science*, *593*(1), 42–65.

Weisburd, D. L. (2008). *Place-based policing.* Washington, D.C.: Police Foundation.

Weisburd, D. & Braga, A. (2006). Introduction: understanding Police Innovation. In Wesiburd, D. & Braga, A. (eds.). *Police Innovation: Contrasting Perspectives.* Cambridge: Cambridge University Press.

Weisburd, D., Mastrofski, S. D., McNally, A. M., Greenspan, R., & Willis, J. J. (2003). Reforming To Preserve: Compstat and Strategic Problem Solving in American Policing. *Criminology & Public Policy*, *2*(3), 421–456.

Weisburd, D., & Neyroud, P. (2011). Police science: toward a new paradigm. *New Perspectives in Policing. Harvard University Executive Session on Policing and Public Safety.*, 23 p.

Welsh, B. C., & Farrington, D. P. (2002). *Crime prevention effects of closed circuit television : a systematic review. Home Office* (Vol. Research S).

Welsh, B. C., & Farrington, D. P. (2009). Public Area CCTV and Crime Prevention: An Updated Systematic Review and Meta-Analysis. *Justice Quarterly, 26*(4), 716–745.

Willis, J. J., Mastrofski, S. D., & Weisburd, D. (2007). Making Sense of COMPSTAT: A Theory-Based Analysis of Organizational Change in Three Police Departments. *Law & Society Review, 41*(1), 147–188.

Wilson, O.W. (1963). *Police Administration.* New York: McGraw-Hill.